This book belongs to:

ABOUT THIS BOOK

From Annie Apple and Bouncy Ben to the Yo-yo Man
and Zig-Zag Zebra, you'll find all the LETTERLAND characters
as well as more than 400 first words in the
LETTERLAND PICTURE DICTIONARY.

On every page there's a useful 'Find the Word List'.
It includes all the words that appear in the picture, whether they
are printed labels or writing on an explorer's map or the
front of Bouncy Ben's book.

Use the list for quick reference or for simple word recognition games.
In the case of vowels, we list short and long vowel sounds separately.

You'll also find some suggested activities, designed to
stimulate the young reader's imagination. They'll help encourage
children to count caterpillars with Clever Cat or help the
Hairy Hat Man find a hidden hippo.

Each page includes lots more opportunities for discussion;
because the more you look, the more you'll discover to talk about.

What's the Doctor doing in the deckchair? He's dozing!
Maybe he's even dreaming about dragons!

Every time you open this book you'll discover something new,
because LETTERLAND makes learning fun.

Letterland™

PICTURE DICTIONARY

Devised and written by Richard Carlisle

Educational Editor: Lyn Wendon

Collins Educational

An imprint of HarperCollinsPublishers

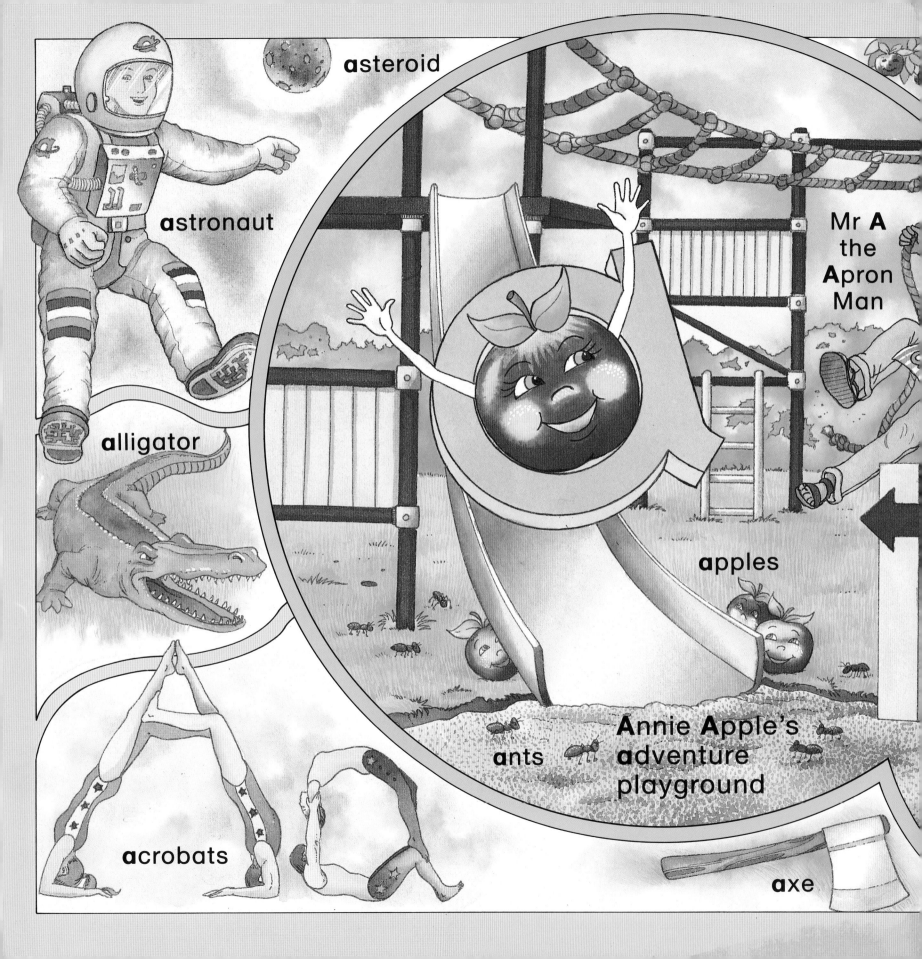

asteroid

astronaut

Mr **A** the **A**pron Man

alligator

apples

ants

Annie Apple's adventure playground

acrobats

axe

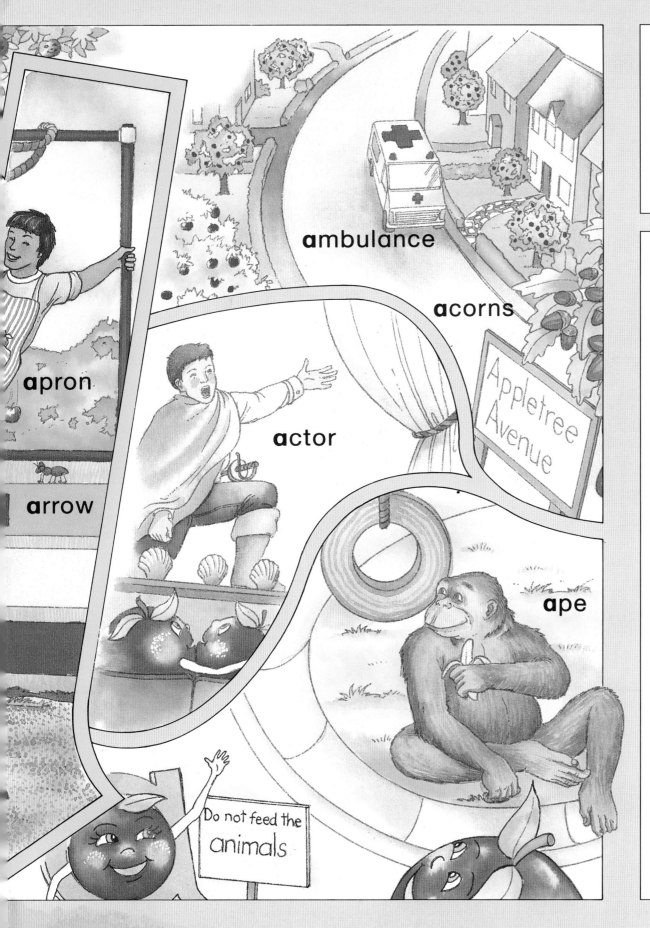

ambulance

acorns

apron

arrow

actor

Appletree Avenue

ape

Do not feed the animals

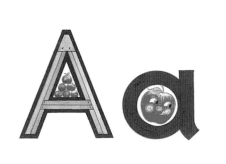

Aa

Find the word

acrobats apples
actor Appletree
adventure arrow
alligator asteroid
ambulance
animals astronaut
Annie Avenue
ants axe
Apple

Mr **A**
acorns apron
ape

Activities

Add up all the apples.

Add up all the ants.

Find an angry animal.

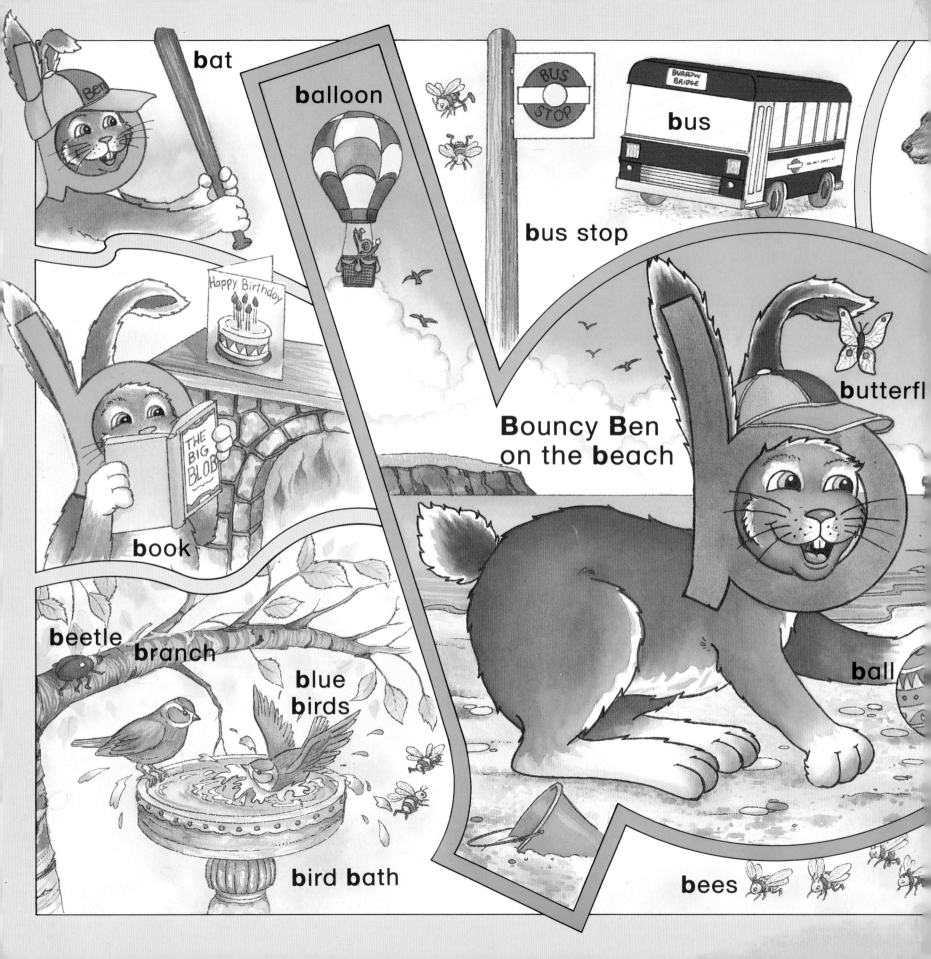

bat

balloon

bus

bus stop

Bouncy **B**en
on the **b**each

butterfl

book

beetle **br**anch

blue
birds

ball

bird **b**ath

bees

bear

breakfast in **b**ed

blanket

boat

bottle

butter

brown **b**read

baked **b**eans

bridge

bicycle

BANG!

Bb

Find the word

baked	**B**irthday
ball	**b**lanket
balloon	**B**LOB
BANG!	**b**lue
bat	**b**oat
bath	**b**ook
beach	**b**ottle
beans	**B**ouncy
bear	**b**ranch
bed	**b**read
bees	**b**reakfast
beetle	**b**ridge
Ben	**b**rown
bicycle	**b**us
BIG	**b**us stop
bird	**b**utter
birds	**b**utterfly

Activities

Count all the bees.

Find something buried on the beach.

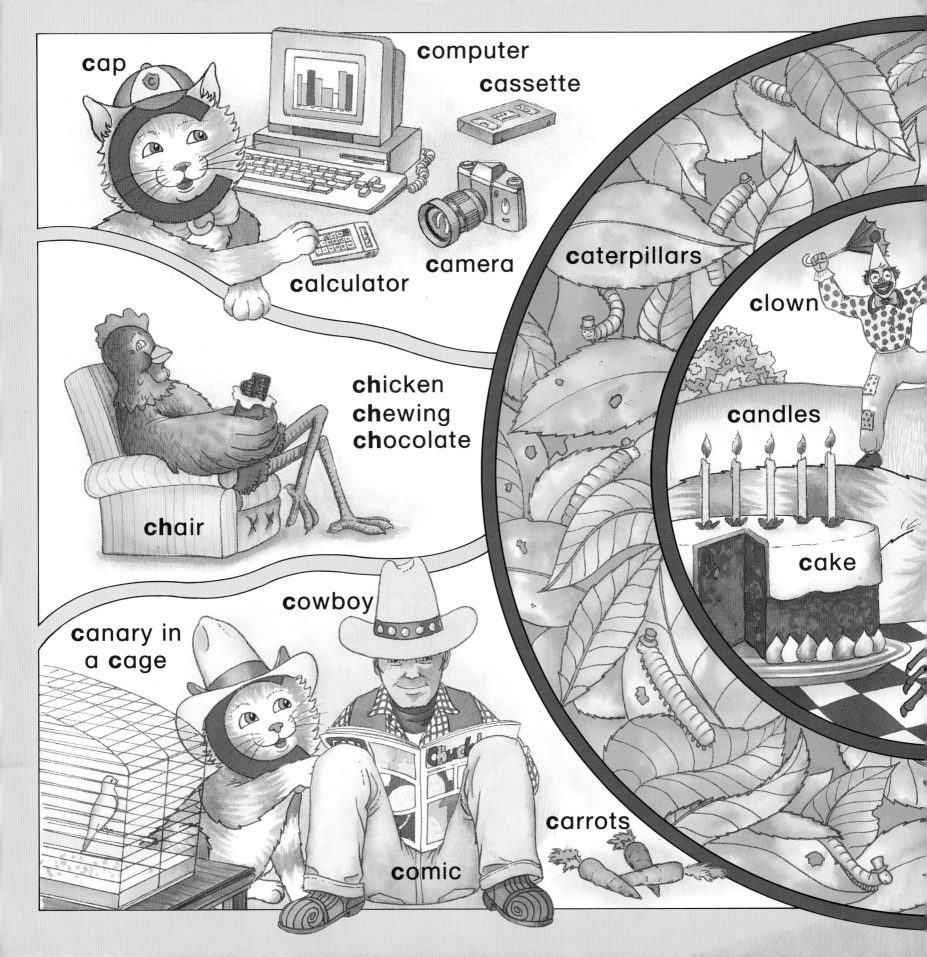

cap

computer

cassette

camera

calculator

caterpillars

clown

candles

cake

chicken
chewing
chocolate

chair

cowboy

canary in
a cage

comic

carrots

clock **c**overed in **c**obwebs

crow

Clever **C**at's picnic

church

camel

claws

crab

crane

crate

car

Find the word

cage	**ch**ocolate
cake	**ch**urch
calculator	**C**lever
camel	**c**laws
camera	**c**lock
canary	**c**lown
candles	**c**obwebs
cap	**c**omic
car	**c**omputer
carrots	**c**overed
cassette	**c**owboy
Cat	**c**rab
caterpillars	
chair	**c**rane
chewing	**c**rate
chicken	**c**row

Activities

Find all the caterpillars.

Count the candles on Clever Cat's cake.

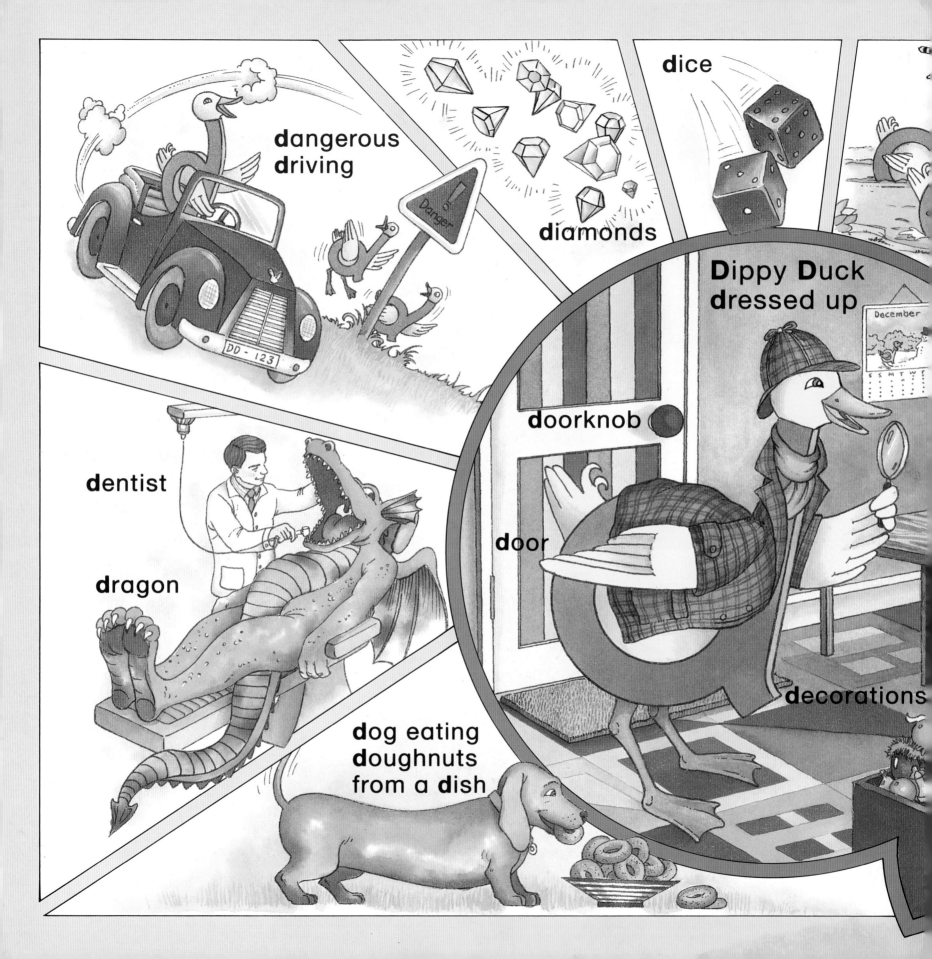

daffodils

dartboard

Doctor in a deckchair

DO NOT DISTURB

desk

doll

drum

drumsticks

diving dolphins

Which **door** is **different**?

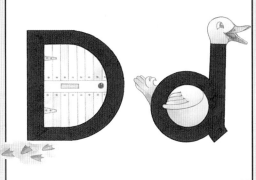

Dd

Find the word

daffodils	**D**O
Danger!	**D**octor
dangerous	
dartboard	**d**og
December	**d**oll
deckchair	**d**olphins
decorations	
dentist	**d**oor
desk	**d**oorknob
diamonds	**d**oughnuts
dice	**d**ragon
different	**d**ressed
Dippy	**d**riving
dish	**d**rum
DISTURB	**d**rumsticks
diving	**D**uck

Activities

Add up the dots on the dice.

Find the dove.

Count the ducks.

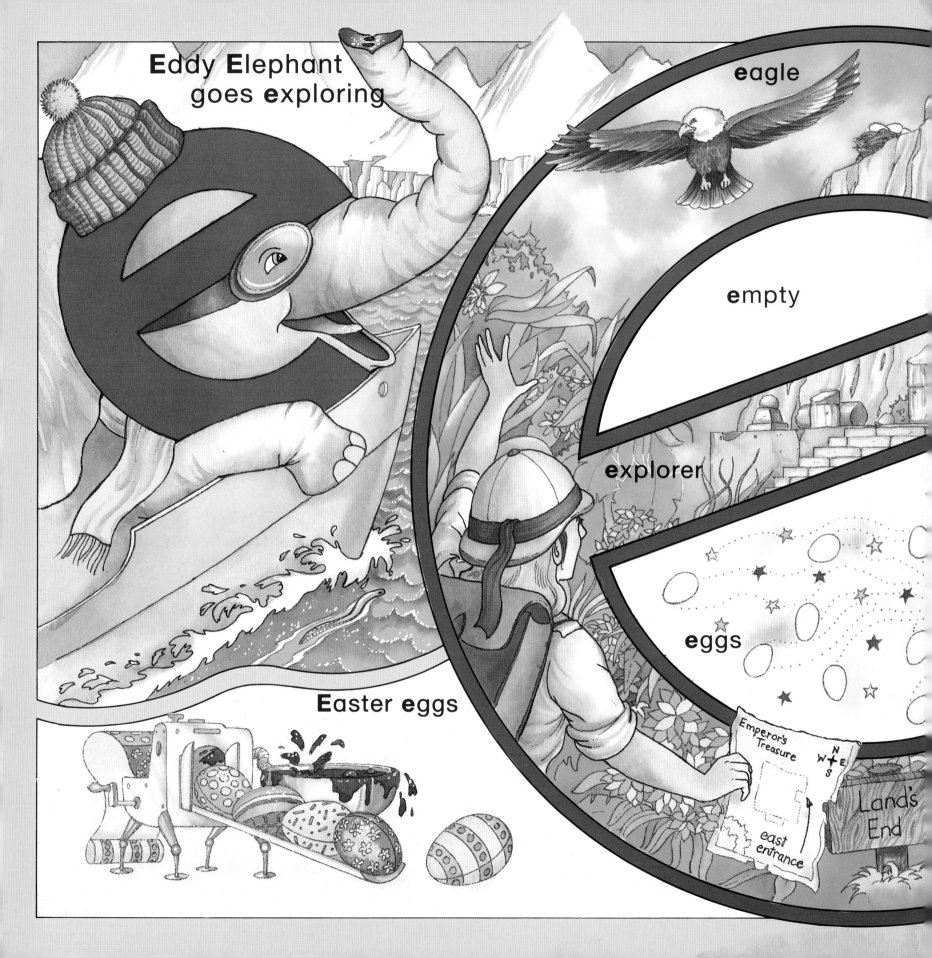

Eddy **E**lephant goes **e**xploring

eagle

empty

explorer

eggs

Easter **e**ggs

Emperor's Treasure

east entrance

Land's End

envelope

E. Elephant
11 Elmtree Estate
Letterland

escalator

entrance

EXIT

explosion

Mr E the
Easy
Magic
Man

Eddy **E**lephant
eating **e**clairs

Ee

Find the word

eclairs   entrance
Eddy   envelope
eggs   escalator
Elephant   Estate
Elm   EXIT
Elmtree   explorer
Emperor   exploring
empty   explosion
End

Mr E
eagle   Easy
east   eating
Easter

Activities

Add up all the eggs.

Find whose treasure
is on the map.

Find the hidden eel.

Fireworks with Fireman Fred

fence

fox

fern

fireflies in the forest

funny face on a flag

factory

field

football

frog

fork

FIRST AID

fifty pence

fire engine

frog

farm

farmer

Find the word

face	Fireworks
factory	FIRST AID
farm	flag
farmer	football
fence	forest
fern	fork
fields	fox
fifty pence	Fred
fire engine	frog
fireflies	funny
Fireman	Fulham

Activities

Count the fireflies.

Count the foxes in the field.

Find a hidden fish.

goal

guitar

glider

gate

grapes

garage

garden

goggles

gloves

grass

game

Golden **G**irl's **g**reenhouse

glass

glasses

gorilla

granny
and
grandad

goat
grazing

goose

ghost

go kart

G g

Find the word

game	**g**oggles
garage	**g**o kart
garden	**G**olden
gate	**g**oose
ghost	**g**orilla
Girl	**g**randad
glass	**g**ranny
glasses	**g**rapes
glider	**g**rass
gloves	**g**razing
goal	**g**reenhouse
goat	**g**uitar

Activities

Count the animals.

Find the grasshopper.

Find the green grapes.

The **H**airy **H**at
Man at **h**ome

hatstand

Home Sweet Home

hair

hand

hill

hamburger

honey

hat

helmet

hay

horse

holly

HOTEL

Hilltop Hotel

hippo

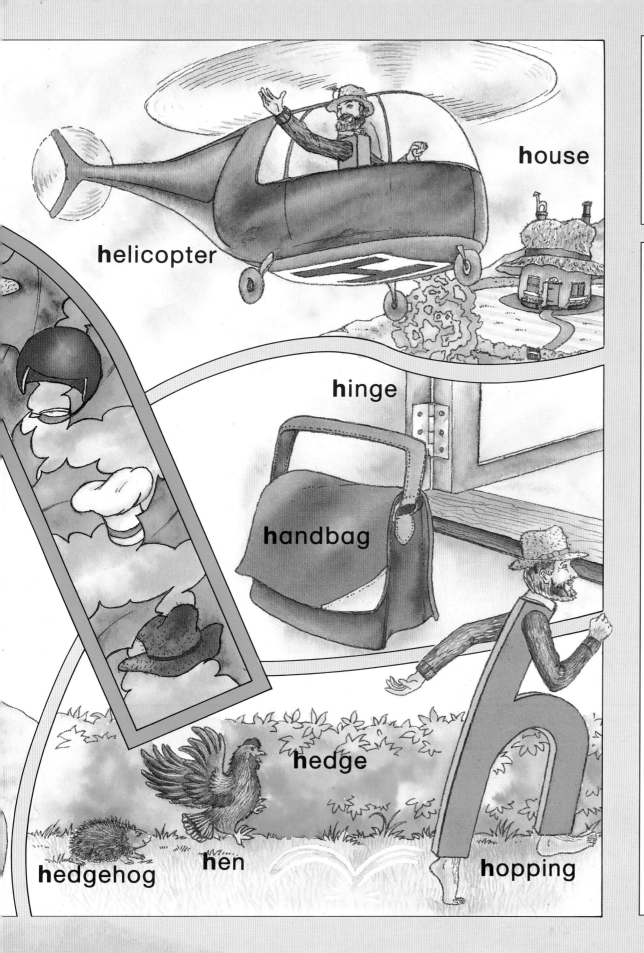

house

helicopter

hinge

handbag

hedge

hen

hedgehog

hopping

Hh

Find the word

hair	**h**ill
Hairy	**H**illtop
hamburger	
hand	**h**inge
handbag	**h**ippo
hat	**h**olly
hatstand	**h**ome
hay	**h**oney
hedge	**h**opping
hedgehog	**h**orse
helicopter	**H**OTEL
helmet	**h**ouse
hen	

Activities

Find the hammer.

Find the hidden hippo.

Count the hats.

Find all the helmets.

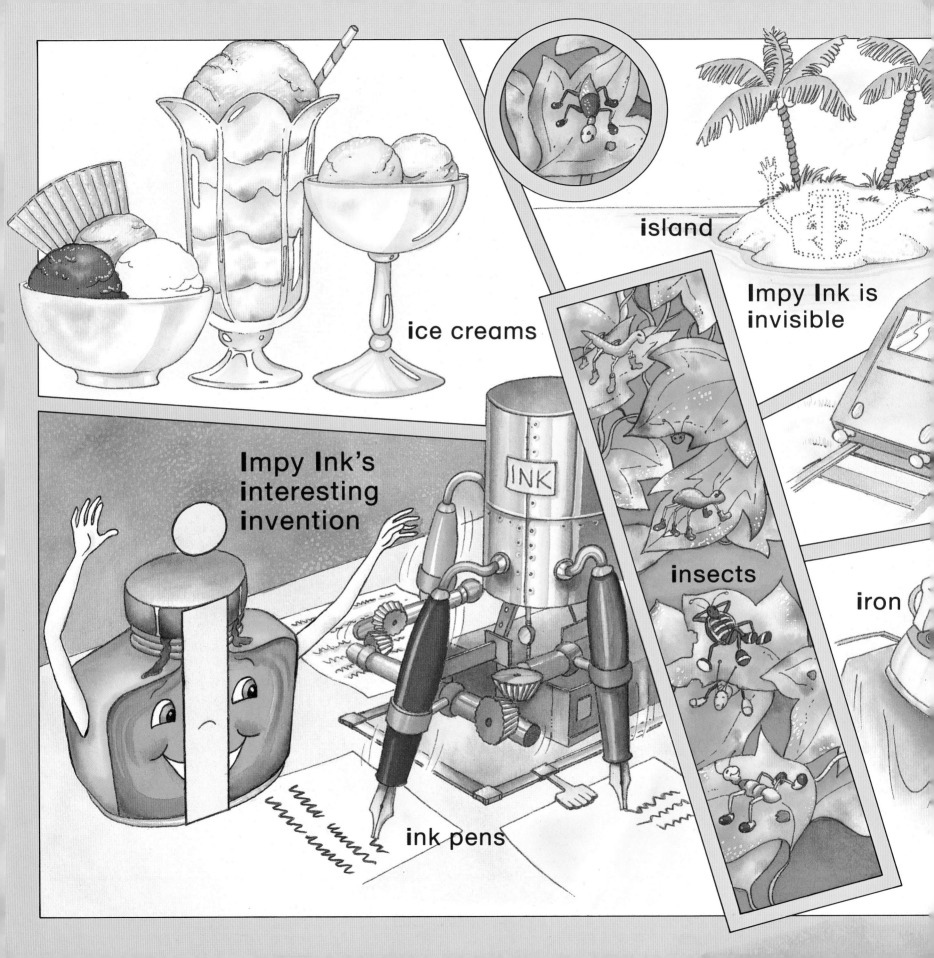

ice creams

island

Impy Ink is invisible

Impy Ink's interesting invention

INK

insects

iron

ink pens

ill

igloo

intercity train

invitation

ice skating

Mr I the Ice Cream Man

Find the word

igloo	interesting
ill	invention
Impy	invisible
Ink	invitation
ink pens	is
insects	
intercity train	

Mr I
ice creams
ice skating
iron
island

Activities

Count the insects.

Count all the ice creams.

Find the invisible islander.

jumping joker

juggling balls

jelly

jacket

jeans

Jumping Jim's
jam machine

judge

jellies

jam jars

jigsaw

jelly
fish

Jumbo **j**et

jewels

jug

jeep

jaguars in
the **j**ungle

Find the word

jacket	**j**igsaw
jaguars	**J**im
jam	**j**oke book
jars	**j**oker
jeans	**j**udge
jeep	**j**ug
jellies	**j**uggling
jelly	**J**umbo
jelly fish	**J**umping
jet	**j**umping
jewels	**j**ungle

Activities

Count the juggling
balls.

Find the hidden jelly.

Find the
jack-in-the-box.

kites

koala

knight
knitting

kennel

Kicking King's
kites

kitchen

kettle

ketchup

key

1 Kilometre to the Kingdom

kittens

kangaroos
kissing

Kk

Find the word

kangaroos
kennel   kingdom
ketchup   kissing
kettle   kitchen
Kevin   kites
key   kittens
Kicking   knight
King   knitting
kilometre   koala

Activities

Find two keys.

Count the kittens.

Count the kites.

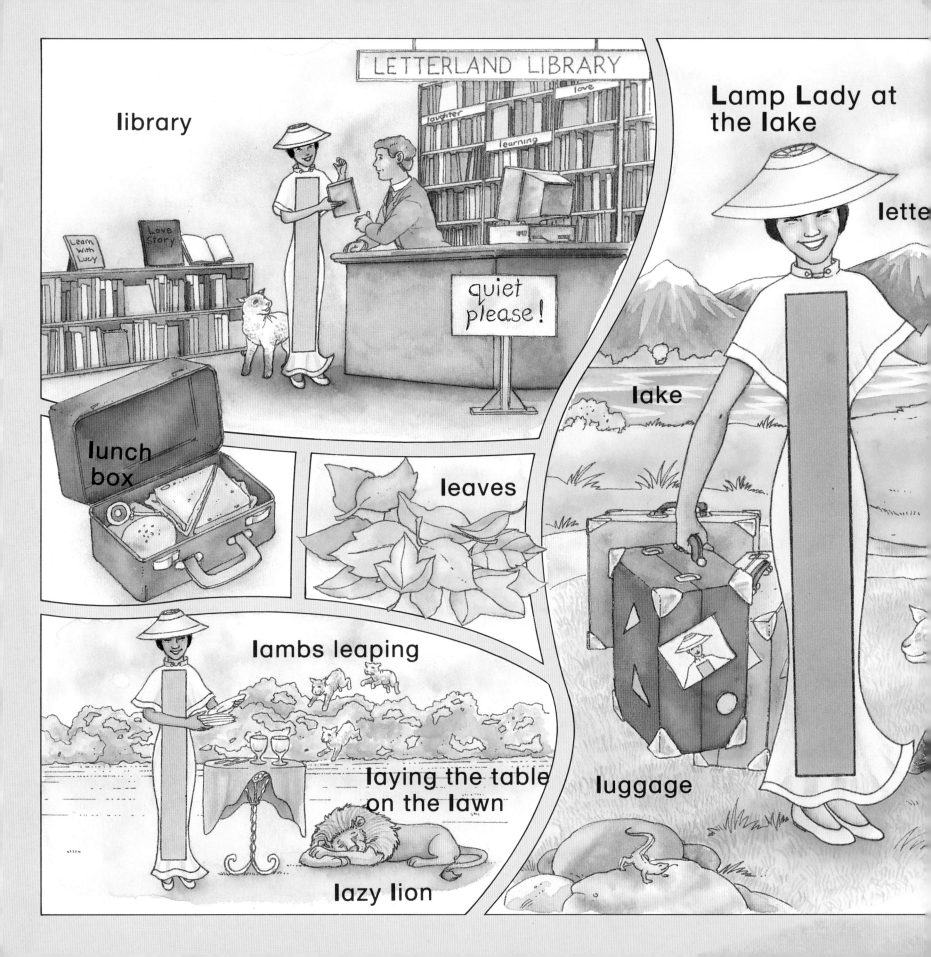

lemons

lightning

lighthouse

logs

adder

lamb

ladder

lifeboat

light
lunch
lettuce
lemon
lime juice

lesson

lorry

Len's Leeks

Ll

Find the word

ladder	lettuce
Lady	library
lake	lifeboat
lamb	light
Lamp	lighthouse
lawn	lightning
laying	lime
lazy	lion
leaves	logs
Leeks	lorry
lemon	luggage
Len	lunch box
lesson	
LETTERLAND	

Activities

Find the lizard.

Count all the lambs.

Look for a lollipop.

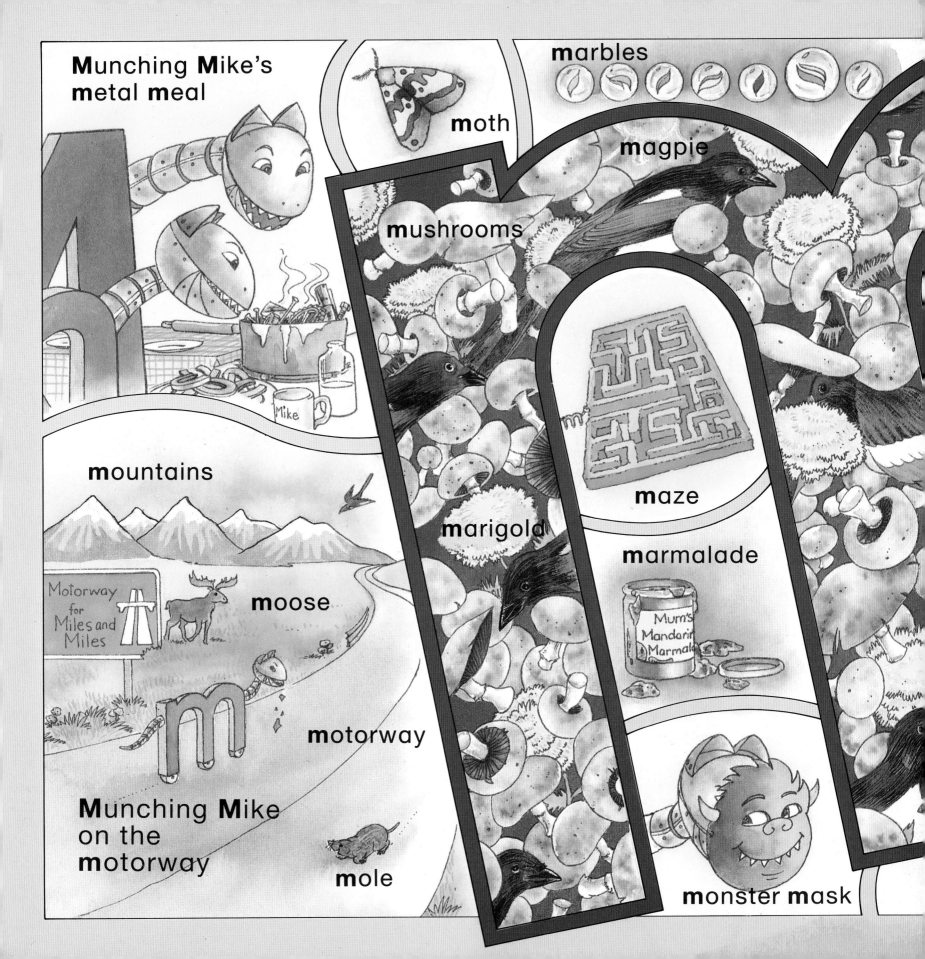

Munching Mike's metal meal

moth

marbles

magpie

mushrooms

mountains

moose

Motorway for Miles and Miles

maze

marmalade

Mum's Mandarin Marmalade

marigold

motorway

Munching Mike on the motorway

mole

monster **m**ask

Mm

map

monkey

magic mirror

model

microphone

music

motorbike

Find the word

magic
magpie
Mandarin
map
marbles
marigold
market
marmalade
mask
maze
meal
metal
microphone
Mike
Miles
mirror
Misty
model
mole
monkey
monster
moose
moth
motorbike
motorway
mountains
Mum
Munching
Museum
mushrooms
music

Activities

Count the magpies.

What is in Munching Mike's meal?

nest

No Entry

No Cycling

Notices

number nine

Naughty Nick's
newspaper

noisy

neighbours

nails

needle

night

nurse

Nn

Find the word

nails	nine
Naughty	No
needle	Noise
neighbours	
nest	noisy
net	Notices
News	number
newspaper	
Nick	nurse
night	nuts
nightly	

Activities

Find the hidden nightingale.

Add up all the nails.

Find the necklaces.

Count all the nests.

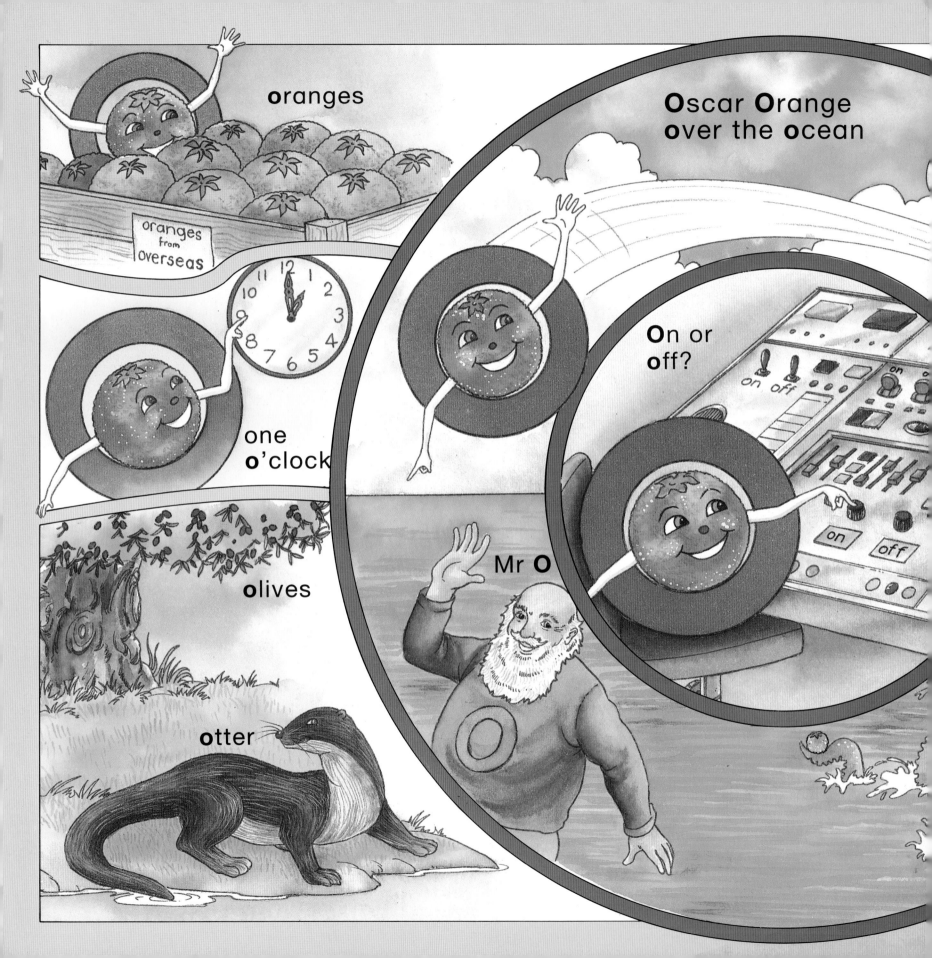

oranges

oranges from overseas

one o'clock

olives

otter

Oscar Orange over the ocean

On or off?

Mr O

octopus

office

Mr. O's office

open

ostrich

Find the word

octopus   **O**range
off   **o**ranges
office   **O**scar
olives   **o**strich
On   **o**tter

Mr **O**   **o**pen
ocean   **o**ver
o'clock   **o**verseas

Activities

Add up all the oranges.

How many legs on one octopus?

Which orange is the odd one out?

pencil

pennies

pears

Poor **P**eter and the **p**ostman

piano

postbox

penguins

palmtrees

postman with **p**arcels

puddle

paws

parrot

pirate

pig

poppies

picture

puppe
paintir

purple **p**aint

pond

playground

pony

Private

picnic

policeman

paper
plane

panda

present

P p

Find the word

paint	**p**ig
painting	**p**irate
palm trees	**p**lane
Pam	**p**layground
panda	**p**oliceman
paper	**p**ond
parcels	**p**ony
parrot	**P**oor
paws	**p**oppies
pears	**p**ostbox
pencil	**p**ostman
penguins	**p**resent
pennies	**P**rivate
Peter	**p**uddle
piano	**p**uppet
picnic	**p**urple
picture	

Activities

Find all the presents.

What are the
penguins playing?

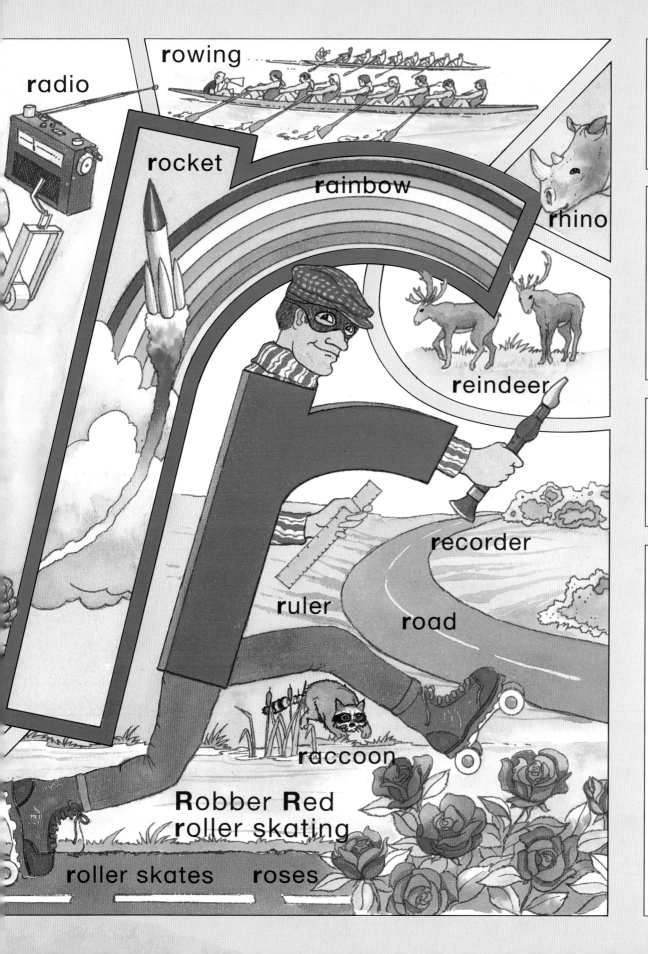

radio

rowing

rocket

rainbow

rhino

reindeer

recorder

ruler

road

raccoon

Robber Red
roller skating

roller skates   roses

Qq

Find the word

qu ads   qu iet
qu ail   qu ill
Qu arrelsome Qu een
qu arters   qu ilt
qu estion   qu iver

Rr

r accoon	r ob
r adio	R obber
r ainbow	r obot
r ecorder	r ocket
R ed	r oller skates
r eindeer	r ope
r eturn	r oses
r hino	r owing
r ing	r uler
r oad	r un

Activities

Find the reeds

Count the roses.

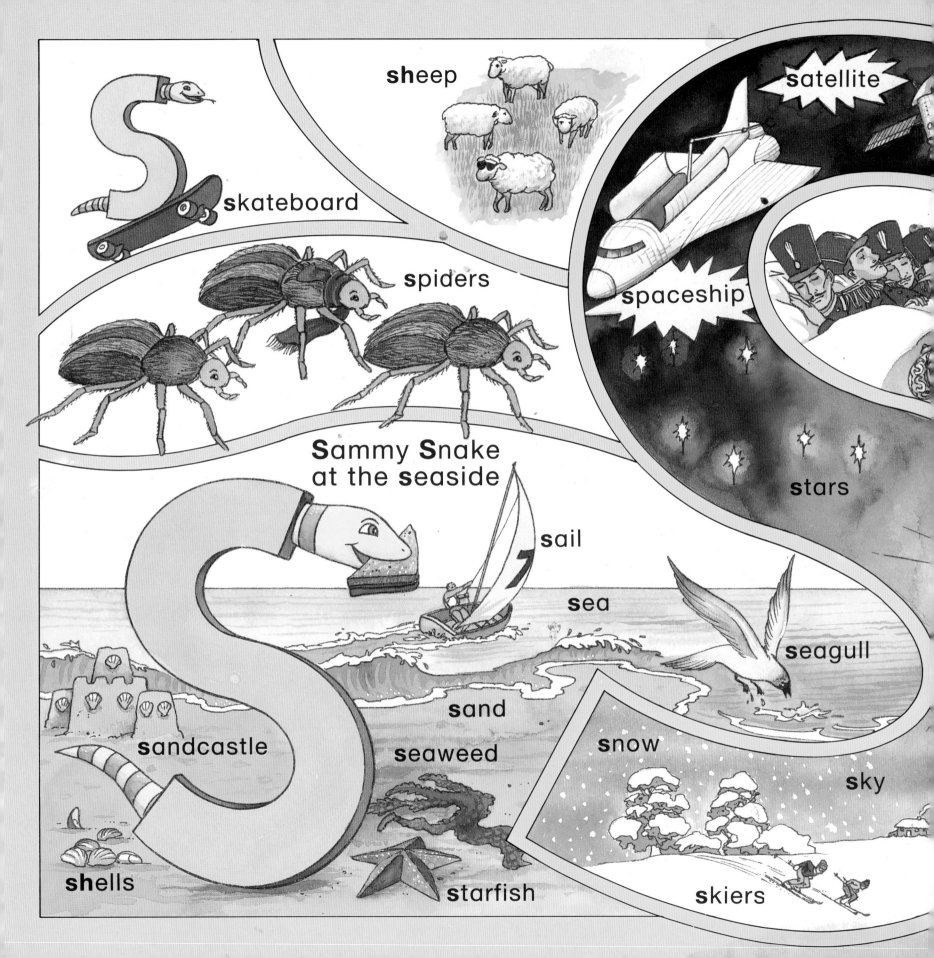

skateboard

sheep

satellite

spiders

spaceship

Sammy Snake
at the seaside

stars

sail

sea

seagull

sand

sandcastle

snow

seaweed

sky

shells

starfish

skiers

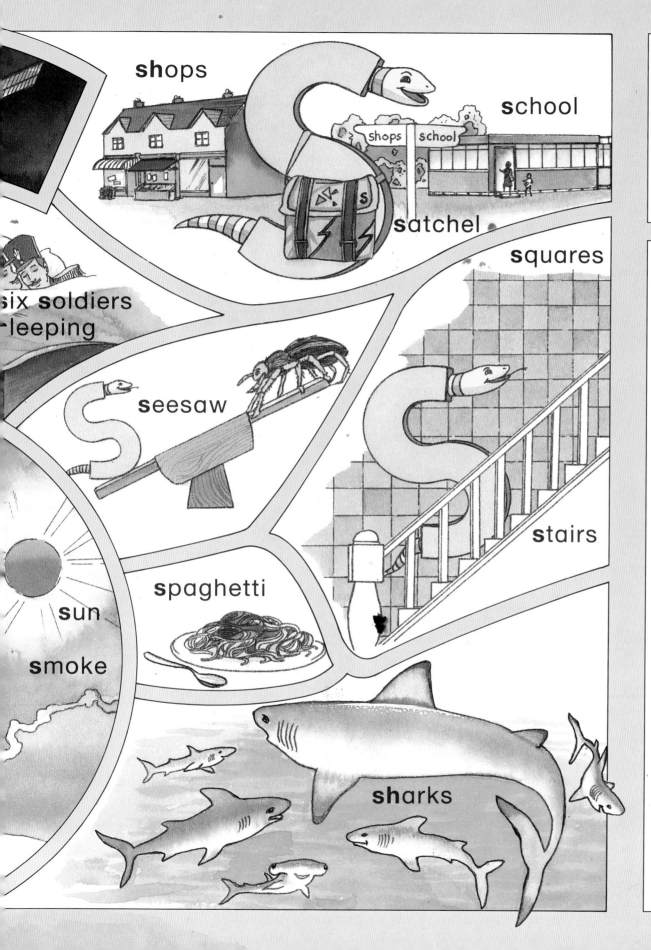

shops

school

satchel

squares

six soldiers sleeping

seesaw

stairs

spaghetti

sun

smoke

sharks

Ss

Find the word

sail	skateboard
Sammy	skiers
sand	sky
sandcastle	sleeping
satchel	smoke
satellite	Snake
school	snow
sea	soldiers
seagull	spaceship
seaside	spaghetti
seaweed	spiders
seesaw	squares
sharks	stairs
sheep	starfish
shells	stars
shops	sun
six	sword

Activities

Count the sharks.

Find the sword.

Add up all the stars.

tiger

train

two tents

taxi

toothbrush

tissue

tap

toothpaste

towel

television

typewriter

teddy bear

toys

tomatoes

Ticking Tess on the telephone

tape recorder

tortoise

ten tadpoles

trees

teapot

tractor

table

Ticking Tom

target

toadstools

Find the word

table	toadstools
tadpoles	Tom
tap	tomatoes
tape recorder	
target	toothbrush
taxi	toothpaste
teapot	tortoise
teddy bear	
telephone	towel
television	toys
ten	tractor
tents	train
Tess	trees
Ticking	two
tiger	typewriter
tissue	

Activities

Count the tomatoes.

Find three tortoises.

Find the traffic lights.

Find the trampoline.

Up

Uppy **U**mbrella
upstairs

unicorn

Mr **U** the
Uniform Man

unhappy

umpire

umbrellas

underneath

volcano

vulture with a violin

vines

viaduct

Vase of Violets

valley

van

Uu

Find the word

umbrellas	**u**p
umpire	**U**ppy
underneath	**u**pstairs
unhappy	

Mr **U**   **U**niform Man
unicorn

Find the word

valley	**V**ince
van	**v**ines
Vase	**v**iolets
Vegetables	**v**iolin
Vet	**v**isitors
viaduct	**v**olcano
village	**v**ulture

Activities

Add up the umbrellas.

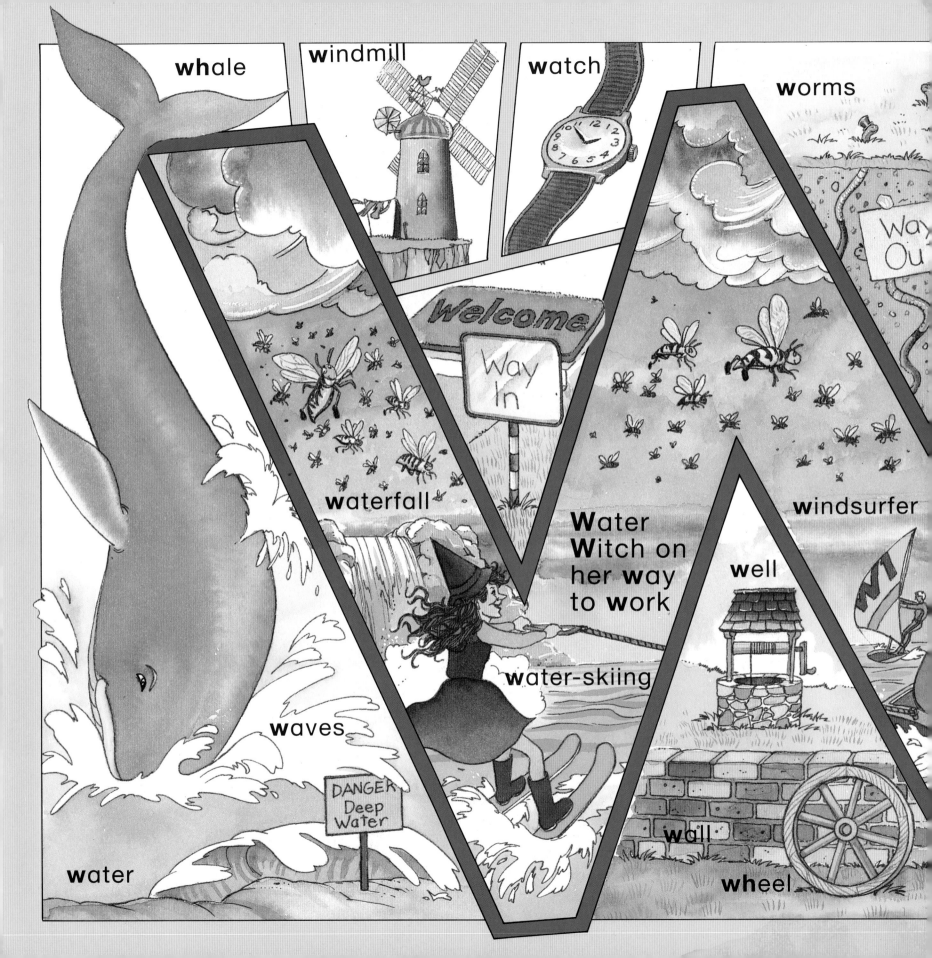

wood

wolf

wasps

walrus

washing machine

wool

wellington boots

Find the word

wall	Wet
walrus	whale
Wash	wheel
washing machine	
wasps	Wild
watch	windmill
Water	windsurfer
waterfall	Witch
water-skiing	
waves	wolf
way	wood
Way In	wool
Way Out	Woollies
Welcome	work
well	worms
wellington boots	

Activities

What is the Water Witch washing?

Who is the wolf waiting for?

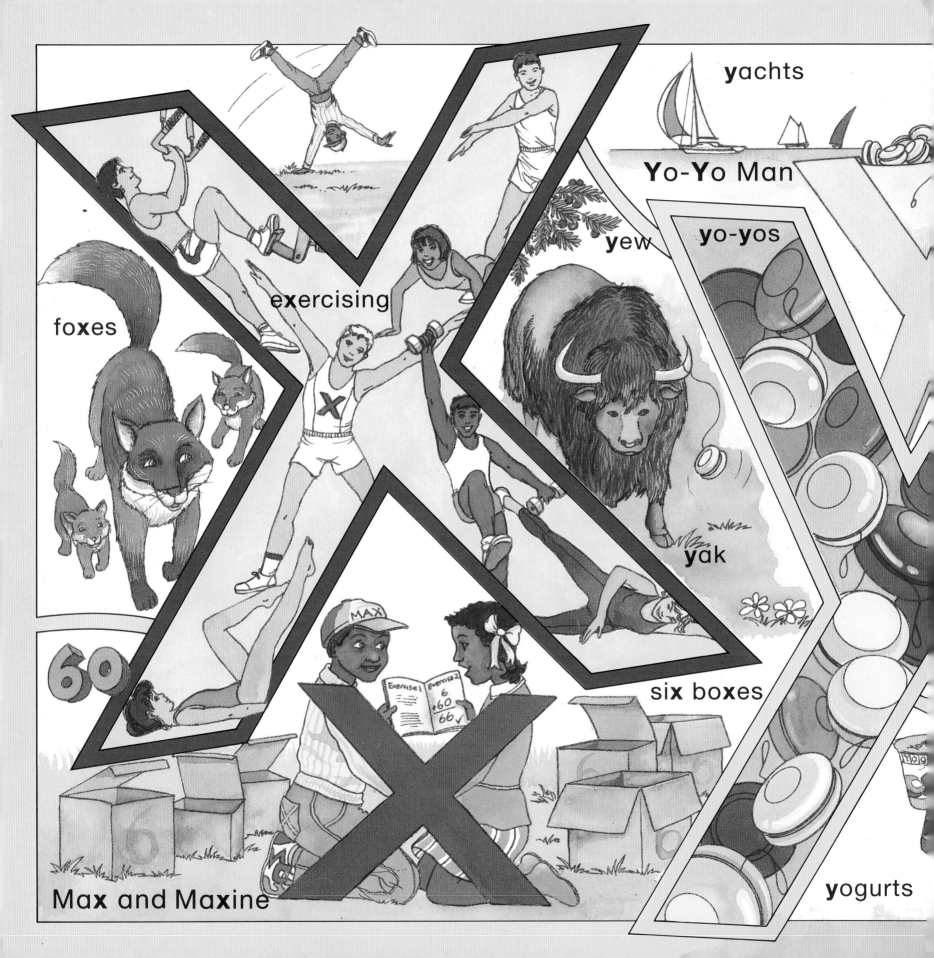

foxes

exercising

Max and Maxine

six boxes

yachts

Yo-Yo Man

yew

yo-yos

yak

yogurts

zoo

Zig
Zag
Zebra

zebra
crossing

zip

boxes   Max
exercising   Maxine
foxes   six

yachts   yo-yos
yak   yogurts
yew   Yo-Yo Man

Zebra   zoo
zebra crossing
Zig Zag   ZOOM!
zip

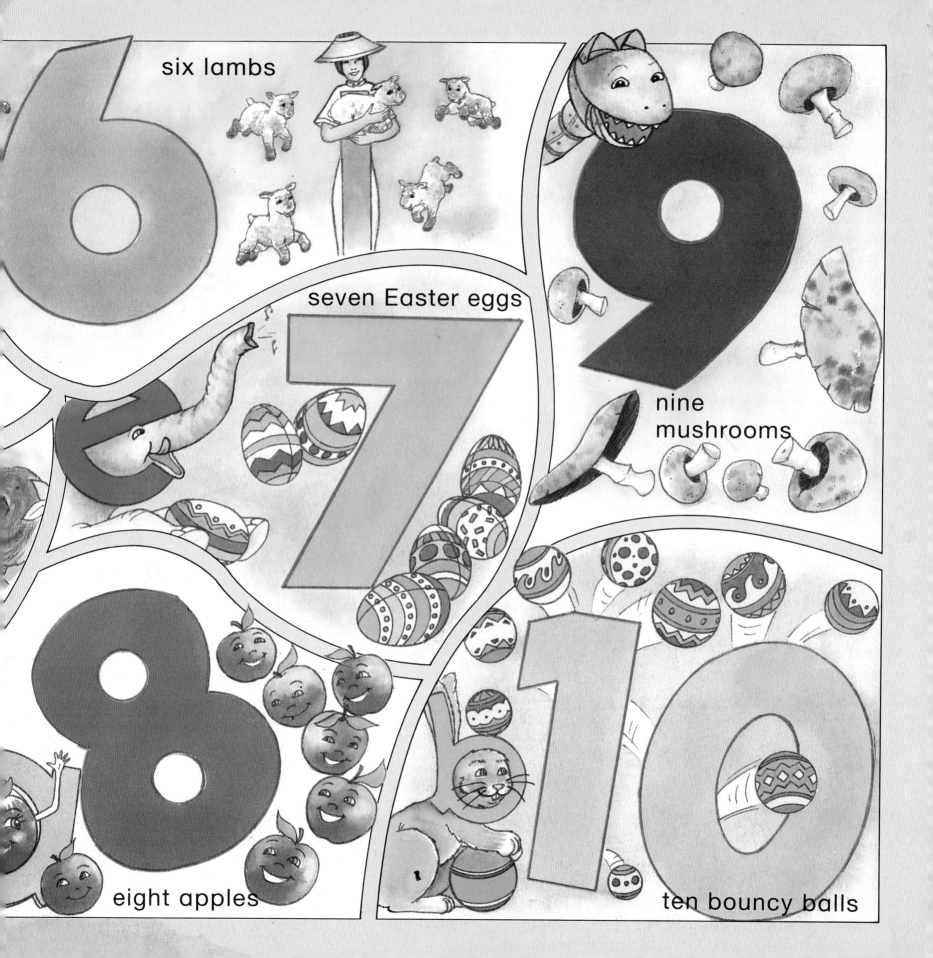

six lambs

seven Easter eggs

nine mushrooms

eight apples

ten bouncy balls

This book is dedicated to Alexander Carlisle — R.H.C.

Published by Collins Educational
An imprint of HarperCollins*Publishers* Ltd
77-85 Fulham Palace Road
London W6 8JB

© The Templar Company plc 1992
Letterland© was devised by and is the copyright of Lyn Wendon

First published by Letterland Direct Limited, 1992.

This edition published 1998 by Collins Educational
Reprinted 1996, 1997

ISBN 0 00 303419 4

LETTERLAND® is a registered trademark of Lyn Wendon.

The author asserts the moral right to be identified as the author of this work.

Printed by Scotprint Ltd., Musselburgh, Scotland.

Letterland Home Learning
HarperCollins publishes a wide range of Letterland early learning books, video and audio
tapes, puzzles and games. For an information leaflet about Letterland call 0181 307 4052.
To order materials call 0141 306 3391.